MW00478326

Myraki Publishing 2018

Maid of Honor
Shit To Do
Before I Do's

Maid of Honor Responsibilities

Congratulations on being selected as the Maid of Honor! Your best friend or relative is trusting you to stand beside her on this most important day!

Below are the duties that the maid of honor is traditionally responsible for. Get together with your bride and adjust this list to what she needs from you.

1. The Bachelorette Party - you are responsible for inviting the ladies, planning the activities, and making sure everything goes smoothly.

2. Help the bride choose her wedding dress and bridesmaid dresses.

3. Plan or help plan the wedding shower with the brides family. Keep a record of the gifts.

4. Attend the rehearsal dinner.

5. Help the bride get ready the day of the wedding and help coordinate events as needed.

6. Help organize the bridesmaids, flower girl, and ring bearer.

7. Be responsible for the brides train and hold the brides bouquet when needed.

8. Give a toast at the reception.

9. Dance with the best man.

10. Be there for your bride throughout the process - she will need your support!

56935964R00046

Made in the USA
Middletown, DE
25 July 2019